First published in October 1992.
Created and produced for Ediciones B, S.A.
by o3 BCN Packagers.
Text: Albert Delmar
Translation: A. Lopes
Illustrations: F. Salvà

© 1992, Ediciones B, S.A.
Rocafort, 104   08015 Barcelona (Spain)

ISBN: 84 – 406 - 3129 - 4
Depósito legal: CO 1019 - 1992
Printed and bound in Spain

Cover:
Pablo Picasso

U.S. & Canada Sole Importer/ Distributor
Trans-National Trade Development Corporation
New York City
Toll Free: (800) 592-2209
Telephone: (212) 922-0450
Fax: (212) 922-0462

Printed by Graficromo, S.A.
Córdoba (Spain)

PICASSO

I do not seek - I find

6

The story of Pablo Picasso

"If you know exactly what you are going to do, why do it? Since you already know, it is no longer interesting. It is better to do something else". (Pablo Picasso)

His complete name was Pablo Ruiz Picasso. He was born in Málaga, a sunny Spanish city on the Mediterranean coast.

Picasso's father José Ruiz was a painter and art professor. But he earned very little money, and more than once he had to pay the rent of the house where they lived with one of his paintings.

Picasso spent the first ten years of his life in Málaga. At school he was so bored that his teacher allowed him to have a pigeon with him so that he would be more entertained and draw it.

José was enthusiastic about how well his son drew and painted. One day when Pablo was 13, José decided to give his son his palette, his paints and his paintbrushes, and he himself never painted again.

At the age of 14, Picasso moved to Barcelona with his family, where he lived for seven years. During this time period, he learned a lot.

In Barcelona Pablo Picasso met a group of older artists. They were advanced, and aware of what was happening in other countries. He had his first exhibition at the *4 Gats (The 4 Cats)*, the café where they usually gathered. Almost all of the works were portraits of his friends.

In 1900 he made his first trip to Paris, where the most important painters of that time lived. He returned several other times. Four years later, he moved there permanently and met Fernande, the woman who would live with him for seven years.

Throughout his entire life, Picasso was very aware of everything that occurred around him: the rapid progress of science and technology, war, peace, festivities, injustice... all of these are reflected in his works.

His feeling are also very present in his paintings. If we pay close attention to the themes, shapes and colors, we can see when he felt happy, sad, lonely, in good company, angry, in love...

In 1901, after the death of a friend, he began his Blue Period, so-called because the paintings from this period are all blue. Picasso felt sad. The people who appear in them are destitute children, abandoned women, old people... Their faces and their bodies reflect the misery that Picasso saw around him. His work, like the world he knew, underwent many drastic changes. He lived and worked very intensively, always experimenting, and opening new paths in art which others would later follow.

Science and Charity

Picasso painted this picture in 1896, when he was 16. Influenced by his father, he entered it into an official art competition. It was the last work that he painted according to the advice of his professors at the art school.

The following year, Picasso wanted to be more independent from his parents, so he moved to Madrid and registered in the San Fernando School. Once there, he never attended a single class. He preferred to spend his time visiting the Museo del Prado, walking the city streets or being with other artists.

Science and Charity (1897)
Oil on canvas, 78,8x99,7 inches
Museo Picasso, Barcelona

The picture shows a sick mother, assisted by a doctor and a nun. It is really a sad scene.

The nun, holding the sick woman's son in her arms, offers her a glass of water. Meanwhile, the doctor takes her pulse. The doctor is a portrait of Picasso's father, José.

12

With this painting, the young Picasso won Honorable Mention at the National Exhibition of Madrid in 1897 and the Gold Medal at the Provincial Art Exhibition in Málaga.

Les demoiselles d'Avignon

Painted in 1907, this picture provoked a big scandal. Nothing like it had been seen before. Even Picasso's friends were horrified by it, and one of them said that it looked like it had been painted with the blows of an axe!

In 1904 Picasso moved to Paris. He felt happy and optimistic. The color pink and circus characters became the focus of his work. This period is known as the Pink Period.

In May of 1906 he traveled to Gòsol, a small village in the Spanish Pyrenees, together with Fernande. In the pictures he painted there, the color pink gives way to ochres and the acrobats to country people.

Les demoiselles d'Avignon (1907)
Oil on canvas, 97,6x93,4 inches
Museum of Modern Art, New York

14

This is the painting that began Cubism. Cubism was a new and revolutionary style of painting, consisting of a new interpretation of space and the use of cubic shapes.

One evening shortly before painting it, a friend had shown Picasso an African sculpture. He spent the rest of the night staring at it in wonder. The next day, his studio was full of drawings similar to the shapes in this picture.

17

There are five women in the room. Someone comes in and they all look at the visitor. On the left there is a woman who just entered the scene.

On the right there is another woman with her back to us. She turns her head - her face looks like an African mask.
Which woman will eat the slice of watermelon?

Guernica

Guernica (1937)
Oil on canvas, 140,4x312,8 inches
Centro Reina Sofía, Madrid

This painting, along with the picture of the doves which Picasso did many years later, has come to symbolize peace and the rejection of war throughout the world.

Picasso painted it in 1937.

In April of that year, during the civil war in Spain, Nazi war planes bombed the small Basque city of Guernica in the north of Spain, destroying it completely and killing and wounding thousands of its population. This bloody act on the part of the German army was part of the military revolt against the Spanish Republic.

General Franco won the war and governed Spain as dictator from 1939 until his death in 1975. During all of those years, Picasso lived in exile, and *Guernica* was left in deposit at the Museum of Modern Art in New York. Once democracy was reestablished, in 1975, it was transferred to Spain.

Picasso painted these images in such a way that they are understood by everyone.

He used white, gray and black, because they are the colors of night and war. A woman cries desperately, carrying her dead child in her arms.

In the center we see a horse, an innocent victim, whinnying in pain. A lance pierces through its body.

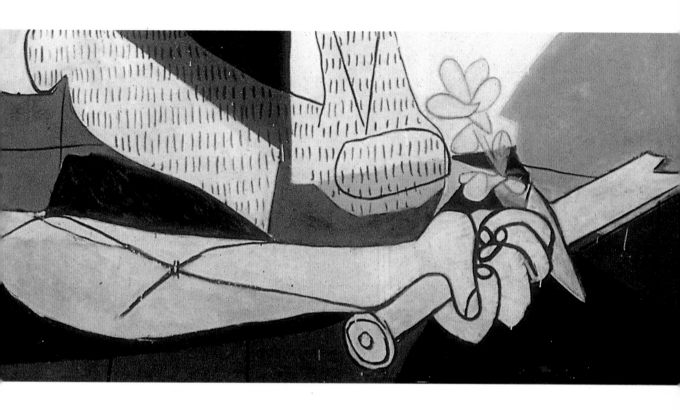

There are people running, fire, panic... On the ground a severed arm holds a broken sword. A flower is coming out of the sword.

26

"I paint the way others write their autobiographies. My canvases, finished or unfinished, are the pages of my diary..." (Pablo Picasso).

Painting, drawing, engraving, sculpture... In a single day Picasso was capable of creating six or seven paintings or dozens of drawings, using different styles and always working with complete freedom.

When he was 72, he met the woman who would be his last wife, Jacqueline. During this last period of his life, he continued to work, surrounded by his wife and friends who came to visit him, as if he were afraid of not having enough time to express everything he wanted to.

Picasso died at the age of 92. It was the month of April. A violent storm of thunder and snow accompanied his funeral.

The old fisherman (1895)
Oil on canvas, 32,8x24,8 inches
Abbey of Montserrat collection, Barcelona

Helpless (1903)
Pastel on paper, 19x16,4 inches
Museo Picasso, Barcelona.

Factory in Hort de Ebro (1909)
Oil on canvas, 21,2x24 inches
Hermitage Museum, St. Petersburg,

Pablo Picasso

1881 Born on October 25th in Málaga, Spain.

1891 He moves to La Coruña with his family, where he attends the School of Fine Arts.

1895 He moves to Barcelona with his family, and attends the School of Fine Arts of the Lonja, where his father is professor.

1896 He paints *First Communion* which is exhibited at the Fine Arts Exhibition in Barcelona.

1897 He paints *Science and Charity*.

1898 He spends some time resting in Horta de Ebro, (Spain). He frequents the Artistic Circle of Barcelona.

1900 He exhibits at "Els 4 Gats" in Barcelona. He paints many portraits and, in October, visits Paris for the first time with his friend Casagemas. He paints *Le Moulin de la Galette*.

1901 He makes a second trip to Paris and exhibits at the Galerie Vollard. He begins his Blue Period with *Big blue self-portrait*.

1904 He moves to the "Bateau-Lavoir" in the Montmartre neighborhood of Paris. He meets Fernande Olivier and creates his first engravings.

1905 He begins his Pink Period and travels to Holland. He paints *The ball balancer*, *The three Dutch girls* and *The acrobats*.

1907 After his stay in Gòsol, in the Spanish Pyrenees, he returns to Paris. He paints *Les demoiselles d'Avignon*.

1909 He spends the summer in Horta de Ebro. He begins the geometric cubism stage. Portraits of Fernande, Vollard, Uhde and Kahnweiler are from this stage. He evolves toward an abstract, baroque cubism.

1912 His first collage: *Still life on wicker chair*.

1914 The Second World War surprises him in Avignon. He evolves toward pointillistic cubism.

1917 He travels to Italy with Cocteau. He opens the Ballet Parade with Diaghilev. He paints *The harlequin of Barcelona*.

Paul the harlequin (1924)
Oil on canvas, 52x39 inches
Musée Picasso, Paris.

The pigeons (1957)
Oil on canvas, 40x32 inches
Museo Picasso, Barcelona.

1921 His son Pablo is born. He paints *The three musicians*, and evolves toward neo-classicism.

1925 He makes contact with Breton and becomes interested in surrealism.

1928 He begins creating sculptures, with Julio González.

1935 His daughter Maya is born. He creates *Minitauromachy* and makes an occasional contribution to the literary world.

1937 He paints *Guernica*.

1940 He evolves toward monstrous and deformed figures.

1945 At the end of the Second World War, he joins the Communist Party.

1946 He lives in Antibes, in the French Mediterranean, with Françoise Gilot. He works with ceramic and lithographs.

1947 His son Claude is born.

1949 His daughter Paloma is born. He paints the peace dove for the Peace Congress poster.

1955-56 He creates the series *The painter and the model*.

1957 He creates the *Tauromachy* engravings, and begins the *The maids of honor* series. New York shows a large retrospective exhibition of his work.

1958 His first linoleum series. He creates a panel for the UNESCO in Paris.

1968 He works on the 347 engravings of the *Crommelinck Suite*.

1970 A large exhibition of his recent works is shown at the Palace of Popes in Avignon, France, which is repeated in 1973.

1973 Picasso dies at the age of 92, on April 8th, in Notre Dame-de-Vie, his house in Mougins, France.

Pablo Picasso's works are principally located in:

Museo Picasso, Barcelona, Spain.

Musée Picasso, París, France.

Museum of Modern Art, Nueva York, Nueva York, U.S.A.

29